TURTLE
COLORING BOOK
FOR ADULTS

△ ART THERAPY COLORING

Preview of Coloring Pages

www.arttherapycoloring.com

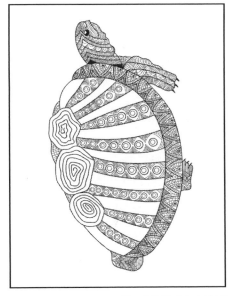

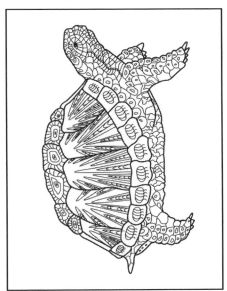

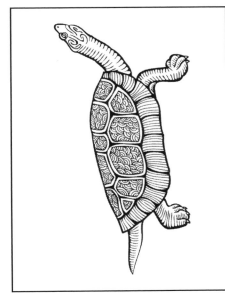

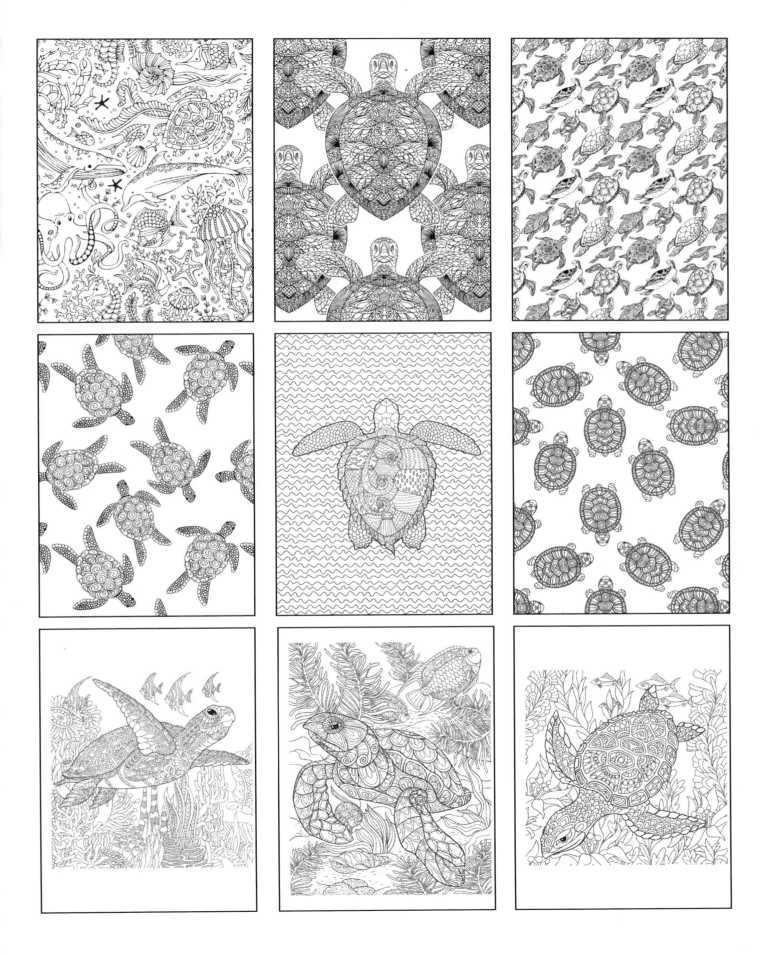

Did You Enjoy Our Coloring Book?

We Want To Hear About It!

Help spread the word about our coloring books! We give 10% of all proceeds from Art Therapy products to benefit cancer patients and their families.

The best way to spread the word is through reviews. We know how busy you are, especially with all of that coloring, but we would appreciate it!

Visit our website at **www.arttherapycoloring.com**

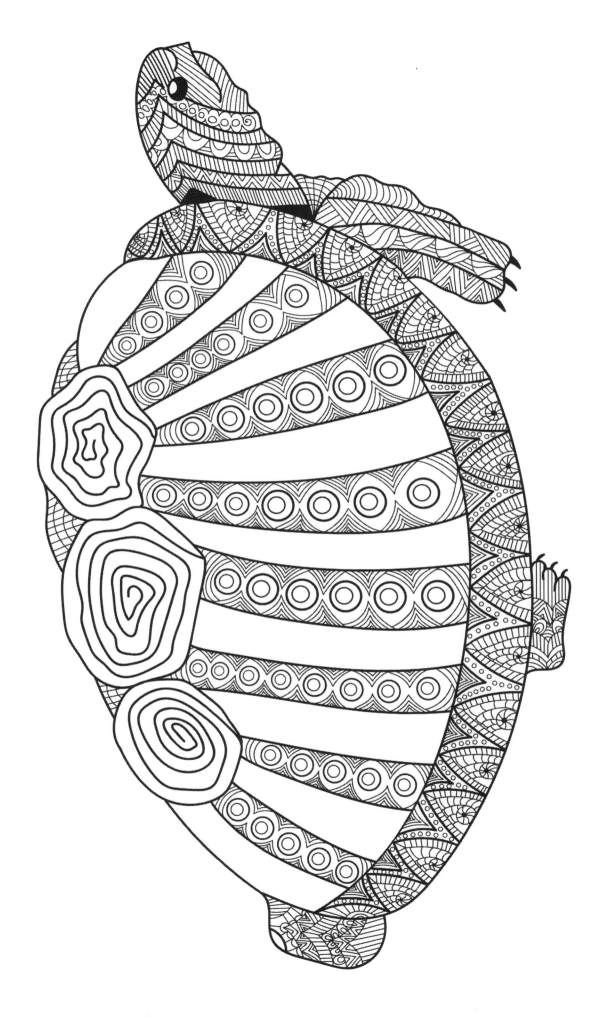

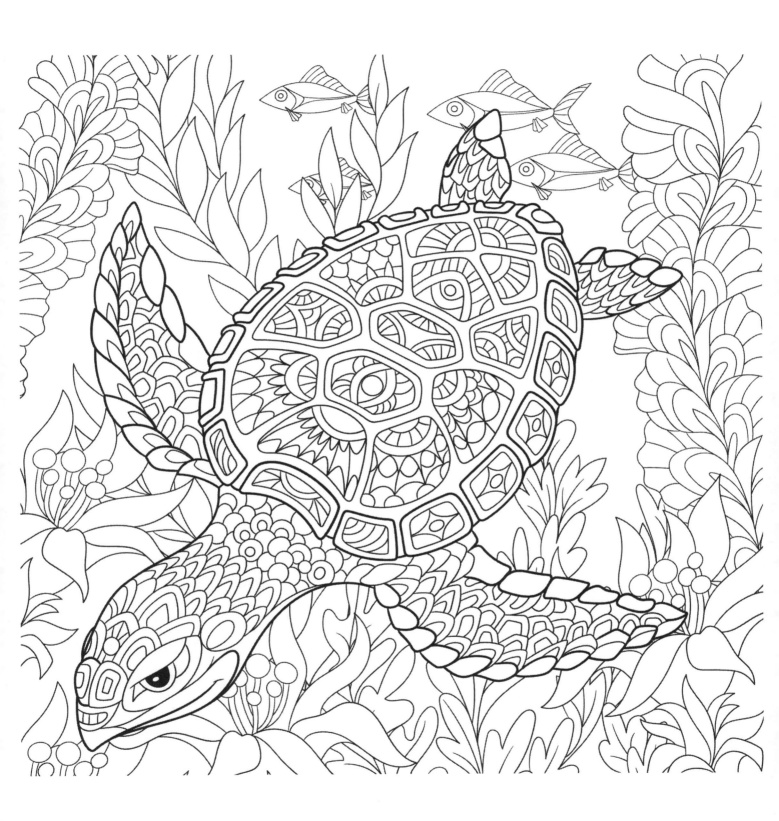

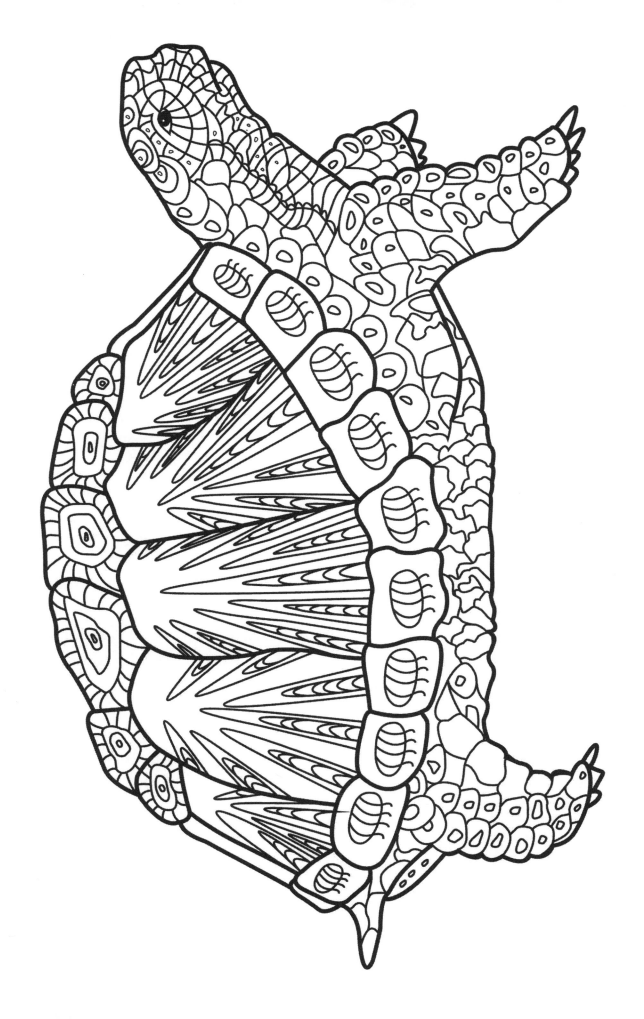

Visit our website at www.arttherapycoloring.com

Get a Free Printable Coloring Ebook!

We've created an exclusive offer for our customers to receive a free Adult Coloring Ebook.

Visit **www.arttherapycoloring.com/freebie** to claim your free coloring book with over 30 new designs that you can instantly print and color!

Over 100 Art Therapy Coloring Books

See our collection of over 100 Art Therapy Coloring Books for Adults, Men, Women, Seniors, Teens, Kids, Boys, and Girls on the following pages.

Coloring Books For Adults

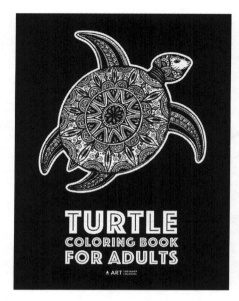

TURTLE
COLORING BOOK
FOR ADULTS
ART THERAPY COLORING

COLORING BOOKS
FOR ADULTS
RELAXATION
Animal Designs
ART THERAPY COLORING

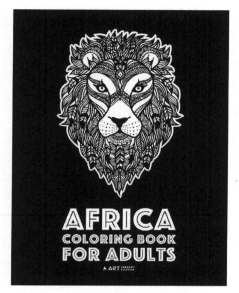

AFRICA
COLORING BOOK
FOR ADULTS
ART THERAPY COLORING

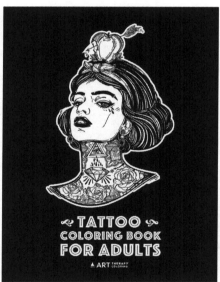

TATTOO
COLORING BOOK
FOR ADULTS
ART THERAPY COLORING

TATTOO
COLORING BOOK
FOR ADULTS RELAXATION
ART THERAPY COLORING

TATTOO
COLORING BOOK
FOR ADULTS
Black Background
ART THERAPY COLORING

Free Spirit

COLORING BOOKS
FOR ADULTS
RELAXATION
Native American Inspired
ART THERAPY COLORING

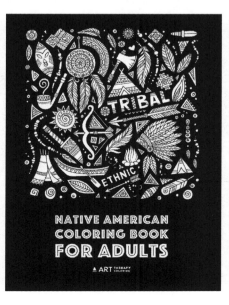

NATIVE AMERICAN
COLORING BOOK
FOR ADULTS
ART THERAPY COLORING

TATTOO
COLORING BOOK
FOR WOMEN
ART THERAPY COLORING

Coloring Books For Adults

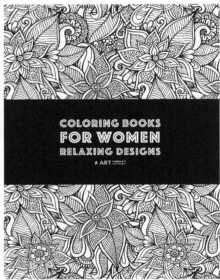

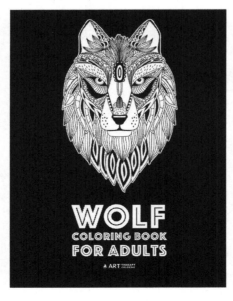

Coloring Books For Men

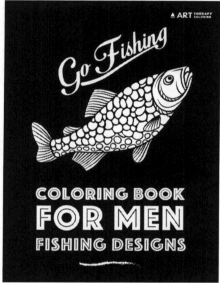

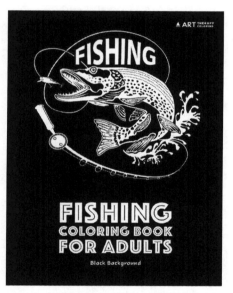

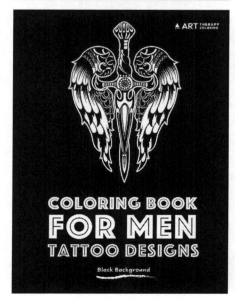

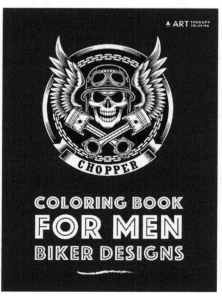

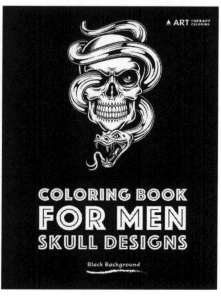

Coloring Books For Seniors

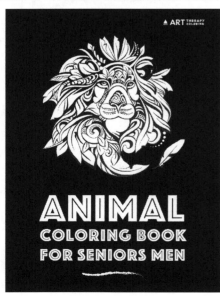

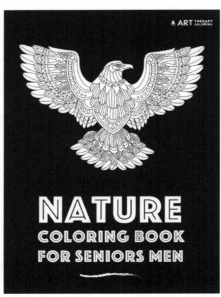

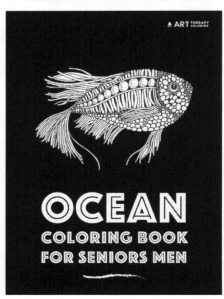

Coloring Books For Girls

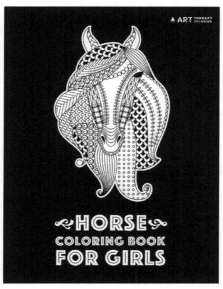

Coloring Books For Boys

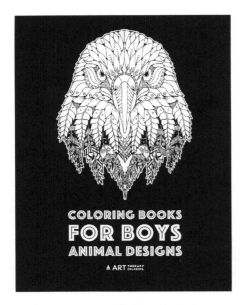

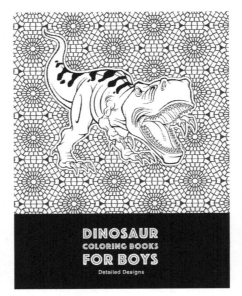

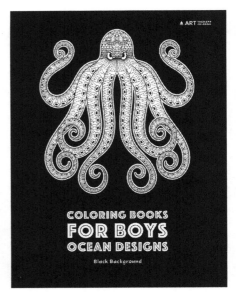

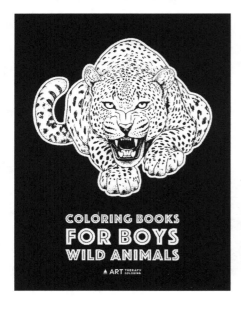

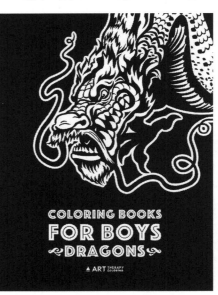

Coloring Books For Kids

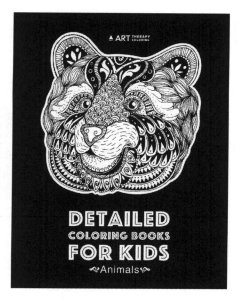

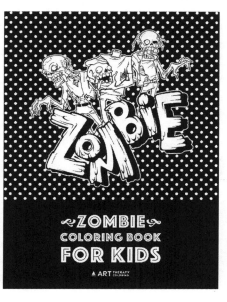

Coloring Books For Teens

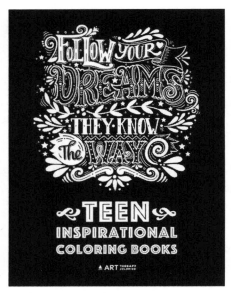

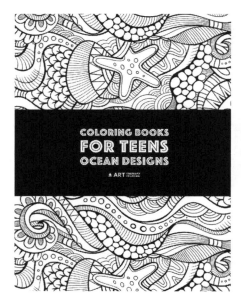

Coloring Books For Teens

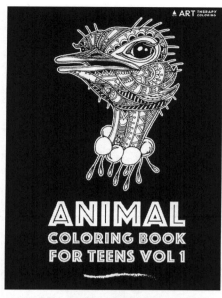

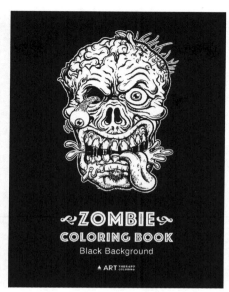

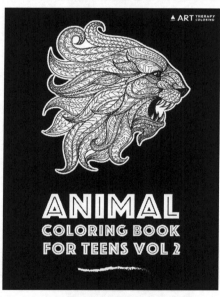

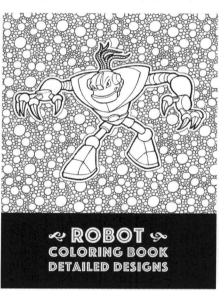

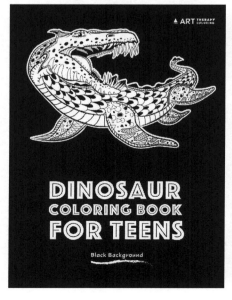

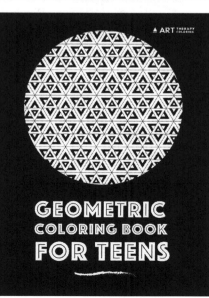

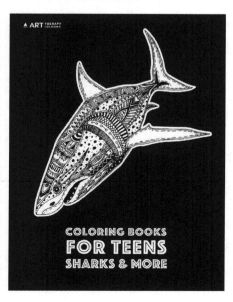

Coloring Books For Teens

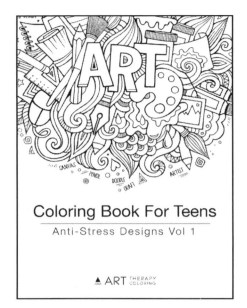

Coloring Book For Teens
Anti-Stress Designs Vol 1

ART THERAPY COLORING

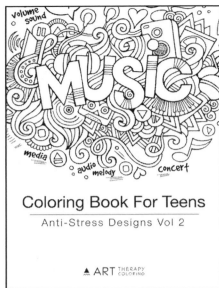

Coloring Book For Teens
Anti-Stress Designs Vol 2

ART THERAPY COLORING

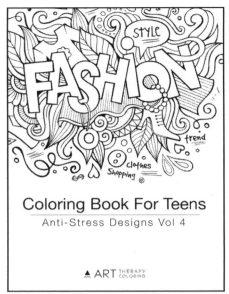

Coloring Book For Teens
Anti-Stress Designs Vol 4

ART THERAPY COLORING

Coloring Book For Teens
Anti-Stress Designs Vol 5

ART THERAPY COLORING

Coloring Book For Teens
Anti-Stress Designs Vol 6

ART THERAPY COLORING

Coloring Book For Teens
Anti-Stress Designs Vol 7

ART THERAPY COLORING

BUTTERFLY
COLORING BOOK
FOR TEENS

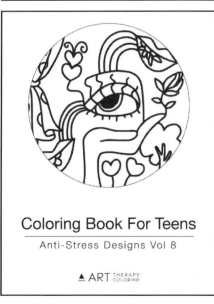

Coloring Book For Teens
Anti-Stress Designs Vol 8

ART THERAPY COLORING

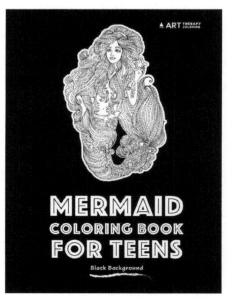

MERMAID
COLORING BOOK
FOR TEENS
Black Background

Coloring Books For Special Occasions

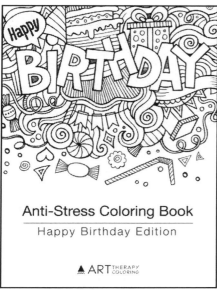

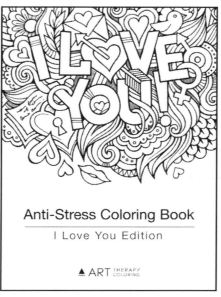

Coloring Books For Christmas

Turtle Coloring Book For Adults

Published by:
Art Therapy Coloring
El Dorado Hills, California
www.arttherapycoloring.com

Shutterstock Images

ISBN: 978-1-64126-073-2

Made in the USA
Lexington, KY
17 September 2018